D0754405

NOTE TO PARENTS

Welcome to Kingfisher Readers! This program is designed to help young readers build skills, confidence, and a love of reading as they explore their favorite topics.

These tips can help you get more from the experience of reading books together. But remember, the most important thing is to make reading fun!

Tips to Warm Up Before Reading

- Look through the book with your child. Ask them what they notice about the pictures.
- Wonder aloud together. Ask questions and make predictions. What will this book be about? What are some words we could expect to find on these pages?

While Reading

- Take turns or read together until your child takes over.
- Point to the words as you say them.
- When your child gets stuck on a word, ask if the picture could help. Then think about the first letter too.
- Accept and praise your child's contributions.

After Reading

- Look back at the things your child found interesting. Encourage connections to other things you both know.
- Draw pictures or make models to explore these ideas.
- Read the book again soon, to build fluency.

With five distinct levels and a wealth of appealing topics, the Kingfisher Readers series provides children with an exciting way to learn to read and wonder about the world around them. Enjoy!

Ellie Costa, M.S. Ed.
Literacy Specialist, Bank Street School for Children, New York

KINGFISHER READERS

level
1

Snakes Alive!

WITHDRAWN

Louise P. Carroll

KINGFISHER

NEW YORK

KINGFISHER
LONDON & NEW YORK

Copyright © Kingfisher 2012
Published in the United States by Kingfisher,
175 Fifth Ave., New York, NY 10010
Kingfisher is an imprint of Macmillan Children's Books, London.
All rights reserved.

Distributed in the U.S. and Canada by Macmillan,
175 Fifth Ave., New York, NY 10010

Library of Congress Cataloging-in-Publication data
has been applied for.

Series editor: Thea Feldman
Literacy consultant: Ellie Costa, Bank St. College, New York

ISBN: 978-0-7534-6846-3 (HB)
ISBN: 978-0-7534-6844-9 (PB)

Kingfisher books are available for special promotions
and premiums. For details contact: Special Markets
Department, Macmillan, 175 Fifth Ave.,
New York, NY 10010.

For more information, please visit
www.kingfisherbooks.com

Printed in China
9 8 7 6 5 4 3 2 1
1TR/1011/WKT/UNTD/105MA

Picture credits
The Publisher would like to thank the following for permission to reproduce their material.
Every care has been taken to trace copyright holders. However, if there have been unintentional
omissions or failure to trace copyright holders, we apologize and will, if informed, endeavor
to make corrections in any future edition.
Top = t; Bottom = b; Center = c; Left = l; Right = r
Cover Shutterstock/Eric Isselee ; Pages 3 Shutterstock/Matthew W. Keefe; 4 Frank Lane Picture
Agency (FLPA)/Michael & Patricia Fogden/Minden; 5 Photolibrary/OSF; 6–7 Shutterstock/
Kruglov_Orda; 7 Shutterstock/J.J. Morales; 8 FLPA/Michael & Patricia Fogden/Minden;
9 Photolibrary/Animals Animals; 10–11 Shutterstock/Ryan M. Bolton; 12–13 Photolibrary/John
Cancalosi; 14–15 FLPA/Dietmar Nill/Minden; 16 FLPA; 17 KF Artbank; 18 & 19 Naturepl/ Kim
Taylor; 20–21 FLPA/Michael & Patricia Fogden/Minden; 22 Shutterstock/EcoPrint;
23 Shutterstock/Audrey Snider-Bell; 23 Shutterstock/Steve Byland; 23 Shutterstock/clkgtr37;
24 Photolibrary/Digital Vision; 25 FLPA/ Danny Ellinger/Minden; 26 Photolibrary/F1 Online;
27 FLPA/David Hosking; 28 FLPA/Heidi & Hans-Jurgen Koch/Minden; 29 Photolibrary/Alaska
Stock; 30-31 Shutterstock/erlire74.

A snake has no arms or legs.

But it moves along!

A snake pushes against a tree.

Up it goes!

Another snake pushes across
the sand.

It moves sideways and forward.

A snake's skin has strong **scales.**

How does the skin feel?

It feels cool and dry.

Snakes come in all sizes.

This is the longest snake.

python

This is one of
the smallest
snakes.

thread snake

Most snakes live
where it is warm.

The sun warms a snake's body.

A snake's tongue moves
in and out of its mouth.

A snake's tongue is like a nose!

It smells the air to find out
if food is near.

Snakes hunt for food.
They eat other animals.

An animal that is hunted
is called **prey**.

Snakes swallow
their food whole.

Most snakes eat prey
that is alive.

Many snakes kill their prey.

Some wind around it and crush it!

Other snakes kill with **venom**.

When the snake bites its prey, venom comes out of its teeth.

These teeth are called **fangs**.

Some snakes eat the eggs of other animals.

The snake swallows the egg.

It cracks
the shell.

Then it
spits the
shell out!

Some animals eat snakes!

Snakes have ways to stay safe.

Some snakes have a **rattle** in their tail.

They shake the rattle to scare other animals away.

Some snakes spit venom.

Some snakes play dead!

Many snakes lay eggs.

The eggs **hatch** and
the baby snakes **slither** out.

Some snakes have live young.

The baby snakes slither off
right away.

A snake grows all its life.

It grows too big for its skin!

The old skin comes off.

New skin is underneath.

A snake leaves its old skin behind.

Then it moves along!

Glossary

fangs the kind of teeth that a snake with venom has

hatch when an egg cracks and a baby animal is ready to come out

hiss a sound a snake makes to scare away other animals

prey an animal that is hunted by other animals

rattle the part of a rattlesnake's tail that can make noise

scales tough, plate-like skin covering a snake's body

slither the way a snake moves

venom a poison that some animals make to kill other animals